DISCONTENTMENT

RESOURCES FOR BIBLICAL LIVING

Lou Priolo, series editor

DISCONTENTMENT

WHY AM I SO UNHAPPY?

LOU PRIOLO

P&R
PUBLISHING
P.O. BOX 817 • PHILLIPSBURG • NEW JERSEY 08865-0817

Unless otherwise indicated, Scripture quotations are from the NEW AMERICAN STANDARD BIBLE®. Copyright © 1960, 1962, 1963, 1968, 1971, 1972, 1973, 1975, 1977, 1995 by The Lockman Foundation. Used by permission.

Scripture quotations marked (NKJV) are from The Holy Bible, New King James Version. Copyright © 1979, 1980, 1982, Thomas Nelson, Inc.

Scripture quotations marked (ESV) are from *ESV Bible* ® (*The Holy Bible, English Standard Version* ®). Copyright © 2001 by Crossway Bibles, a publishing ministry of Good News Publishers. Used by permission. All rights reserved.

Scripture quotations marked (NIV) are from the HOLY BIBLE, NEW INTERNATIONAL VERSION®. NIV®. Copyright © 1973, 1978, 1984 by International Bible Society. Used by permission of Zondervan Publishing House. All rights reserved.

Italics within Scripture quotations indicate emphasis added.

ISBN: 978-1-59638-413-2 (pbk)
ISBN: 978-1-59638-564-1 (ePub)
ISBN: 978-1-59638-563-4 (Mobi)

Eye image © istockphoto.com / olgach

Printed in the United States of America

PERHAPS YOU'VE NEVER thought of discontentment as a root cause for your unhappiness, but as a Christian, you really should. It just might be that you have underestimated the misery that this common sin can produce. Many of those who seek my advice for any number of problems unknowingly struggle with this issue. It is *the* underlying problem for many.

What is the opposite of contentment?

"Why, that would be discontentment, of course."

Sure, but what does the Bible set over against contentment? I don't think you will find the word *discontentment* in too many concordances.

"I guess you're right. So what is it?"

How about *covetousness*? "Let your conduct be without *covetousness*; *be content* with such things as you have. For He Himself has said, 'I will never leave you nor forsake you'" (Heb. 13:5 NKJV, quoting Josh. 1:5; cf. Eccl. 5:10).

It is covetousness (our inordinate desire to have more than what God has seen fit to give us) that makes us discontent. Jesus warns, "Take heed and beware of covetousness, for one's life does not consist in the abundance of the things he possesses" (Luke 12:15 NKJV). Jesus is saying that we need to be on guard against our sinful desires to have more than what has been appointed for us to have. Our good, sovereign, loving, and wise heavenly Father knows much better than we do what we need to glorify and enjoy him now and forever. He knows what will make us happy. He knows how much of a good thing we can handle and how much of it will tempt us to sin. We don't fully comprehend these things, although we often think we do. In his classic book

5

The Art of Divine Contentment, Thomas Watson makes some interesting points:

> God sees, in His infinite wisdom, that the same condition is not suitable for all; that which is good for one, may be bad for another; one season of weather will not serve all men's occasions, one needs sunshine, another rain; one condition of life will not fit every man, no more than one suit of apparel will fit every body; prosperity is not fitting for all, neither is adversity. If one man is brought low, perhaps he can bear it better than another can; he has a greater supply of grace, more faith and patience. . . . Another man is seated in an eminent place of dignity; he is better suited for it; perhaps it is a place that requires a greater measure of judgment, which every one is not capable of; perhaps he can use his estate better, he has a public [open] heart as well as a public place [open home]. The wise God sees that condition to be bad for one, which is good for another; hence it is He who places men in different orbs and spheres; some higher, some lower. One man desires health, God sees sickness is better for him; God will work health out of sickness, by bringing the body of death, into a consumption. Another man desires liberty, God sees restraint better for him; he will work his liberty by restraint; when his feet are bound, his heart shall be most enlarged. Did we believe this, it would give a check to the sinful disputes and quibbles of our hearts: shall I be discontented at that which is enacted by a decree, and ordered by a providence? Am I going to be a [devoted] child or a rebel?[1]

As we will see, the New Testament writers repeatedly address this issue.

Now, just in case I haven't yet convinced you of the tremendous scope of this problem, perhaps a peek into your own heart might persuade you. Here is a little test you can take that will

---

1. Thomas Watson, *The Art of Divine Contentment* (London: L. B. Seeley and Sons, 1829), 39–40 (paraphrased).

give you a general idea of the extent to which you struggle with discontentment.

Biblical Contentment Inventory

Respond to each of the following twenty-five statements, using the rating scale below according to the frequency of each occurrence.

RATING SCALE	POINTS
NEVER (HARDLY EVER)	4
SELDOM	3
SOMETIMES	2
FREQUENTLY	1
ALWAYS (ALMOST ALWAYS)	0

1. I am prone to murmur and complain when things in my life do not go as I wish.
2. I tend to worry and fret when I am faced with the loss of some temporal possession.
3. I get distracted and have difficulty focusing on my God-given responsibilities when things do not go according to my expectations.
4. I give in to discouragement rather than trust God when it seems that my hopes and desires are not going to be fulfilled.
5. I am more motivated by how the things I want will please me than how they will glorify God.
6. I am willing to sin in order to get what I want.
7. I get angry or have some other sinful attitude if I do not get what I want.
8. I spend most of my spare thought time every day thinking about material things rather than eternal things.
9. I derive more pleasure from my thoughts about worldly plenty than I do from my thoughts of Christ, his Word, heaven, and spiritual things.

10. I become more grieved over the loss or lack of my material possessions than I do over my sin.

11. I talk more about being prosperous in the world than I do about being prosperous in God's eyes.

12. I console myself, when in trouble or distress, more with thoughts and desires of worldly provisions than with trust in God and hope of heaven.

13. I am more grateful to God and man for a gift of temporal significance (money, jewelry, clothing) than for a gift of spiritual significance (biblical counsel, books, instruction).

14. I am more concerned with providing for the physical well-being of my family than with their spiritual well-being.

15. I invest a greater portion of my income in worldly pleasures or unnecessary creature comforts than I do in the kingdom of God.

16. I become angry in undesirable circumstances that I cannot control.

17. I become angry when someone in a position of authority asks me to do something that I don't want to do and I can't persuade that authority to change his or her mind.

18. I become anxious when I think people are rejecting me, even though I know I've done nothing to offend them.

19. I enjoy certain recreational/diversionary activities so much that I wonder whether I could really be happy if I had to live without them.

20. I wish others would treat me with much more respect than they usually do.

21. I get bored with my life and wish it were more interesting or exciting.

22. I wish I could enjoy certain sinful activities without feeling guilty.

23. I become irritable when people do things that cut into my free time.

24. I wish I could live a life of ease with more pleasure than work.

25. I think that I have missed God's best for my life or that I will always be trapped in my present circumstances.

By adding up your total points based on 100 percent, you will get a general idea of how content you really are.[2] This should give you some idea of how *discontent* you are. If you scored from 91 to 100, you have no problem with discontentment. (You may have a problem with *dishonesty!*) If you scored from 81 to 90, you are mildly discontent. If your score was from 71 to 80, there are probably some areas of discontentment in your life that need attention. If you scored in the 61–70 range, you may be what the Bible refers to as a "covetous man" (Eph. 5:5). If your sum is 60 or below, you are in danger of becoming a full-fledged idolater.

What I will attempt to do next is to unpack what it means to be content by providing you with seven working definitions of *contentment*. This is intended to enable you to better diagnose any discontentment that may be lurking around in the recesses of your heart. These definitions are like pieces of hard candy. Unlike soft candies (M&Ms, for example, which "melt in your mouth"), hard candies must be slowly dissolved in one's mouth.[3] They (and the biblical truths from which they were derived) are best savored rather than chewed. Similarly, a lot of glorious flavor is compacted into each biblical concept—which I will not have time to describe in its entirety (even if I could).[4]

2. Obviously, this inventory is not a scientifically normed instrument. Because the questions were developed from biblical constructs, persons taking the test are being compared more closely to the character of Jesus Christ than to the character of those in our secular society.

3. When was the last time you had a Jolly Rancher? Maybe it's been awhile. But chances are, whenever it was, you didn't chew it but rather sucked the life out of it as it made its way from the left side of your mouth to the right side, where it no doubt got stuck to a few of your teeth and had to be dislodged with your tongue before it made its way back to another part of your mouth. All the while, you were savoring its flavor as it was slowly dissolving into a piece so small and fragile that you decided to shatter it into tiny fragments that immediately disintegrated on your tongue.

4. If you do not have a sweet tooth, you might want to think of these definitions in terms of a pizza pie that has been cut into seven slices. Each slice differs slightly in size and content, but all slices must be baked together for the pie to be correctly prepared.

1. Contentment is realizing [5] that God has already provided everything that a person needs to glorify and enjoy him.

When I first learned the truth contained in this concept, it was stated something like this: "Contentment is realizing that God has already provided everything I need for my present happiness."[6] This definition is, of course, factual. But I decided to align it more closely to the Westminster Catechism, because in so doing, it now represents not only the *blessedness* of our primary purpose in life (to enjoy God), but also our *responsibility* (to glorify him).

The Greek noun translated as *contentment* in 1 Timothy 6:6 means "self-sufficiency."

"How do you get contentment out of that?" you may wonder.

The idea is a God-dependent self-sufficiency—that is, a kind of self-sufficiency that is dependent on God's abundant resources rather than one's own. If you are content, you have, by God's grace, the *inner resources* to face living without those *outward things* that others depend on for their happiness. If you are truly content, you will be self-sufficient in a God-dependent sort of way. You will not depend on any *outward resources* for your source of strength, comfort, help, or hope; you will seek nothing more than what God has graciously given you, knowing that he has provided everything you need to enjoy, love, serve, and glorify him.

> And God is able to make all grace abound toward you, that you, *always having all sufficiency in all things*, may have an abundance for every good work. (2 Cor. 9:8 NKJV)

> Not that I speak from want, for I have learned to be content in whatever circumstances I am. I know how to get along with

5. To *realize* something is to make it real, to comprehend it fully.

6. I am indebted to the Institute in Basic Life Principles for the first two definitions of contentment developed in this booklet. The original wording of this first definition is from their Character Bookshelf Series game *Character Clues* (Oak Brook, Illinois: Institute in Basic Youth Conflicts, 1974).

humble means, and I also know how to live in prosperity; in any and every circumstance I have learned the secret of being filled and going hungry, both of having abundance and suffering need. I can do all things *through Him who strengthens me.* (Phil. 4:11–13)

What exactly are these inner resources? Below are some of the more prominent ones.

The Holy Spirit. "He would grant you, according to the riches of His glory, to be strengthened with power through His Spirit in the inner man" (Eph. 3:16).

The internalized Word of God. "And take the helmet of salvation, and the sword of the Spirit, which is the word of God" (Eph. 6:17).

Faith in the living sovereign God. "In addition to all, [take] up the shield of faith with which you will be able to extinguish all the flaming arrows of the evil one" (Eph. 6:16).

Prayer. "With all prayer and petition pray at all times in the Spirit" (Eph. 6:18).

Truth and wisdom. "He . . . walks with integrity, and works righteousness, and speaks truth in his heart" (Ps. 15:2). "Behold, You desire truth in the innermost being, and in the hidden part You will make me know wisdom" (Ps. 51:6). "In [Christ] are hidden all the treasures of wisdom and knowledge" (Col. 2:3).

A thankful heart. "Be anxious for nothing, but in everything by prayer and supplication with thanksgiving let your requests be made known to God. And the peace of God, which surpasses all comprehension, will guard your hearts and your minds in Christ Jesus" (Phil. 4:6–7).

Hope. "Now may the God of hope fill you with all joy and peace in believing, so that you will abound in hope by the power of the Holy Spirit" (Rom. 15:13). "Therefore we do not lose heart, but though our outer man is decaying, yet our inner man is being renewed day by day. For momentary, light affliction is producing for us an eternal weight of glory far beyond all comparison" (2 Cor. 4:17–18).

A disciplined mind (self-control). "For God has not given us a spirit of timidity, but of power and love and discipline" (2 Tim. 1:7).

The fruit of the Spirit. "But the fruit of the Spirit is love, joy, peace, patience, kindness, goodness, faithfulness, gentleness, self-control; against such things there is no law" (Gal. 5:22–23).

Christian character. "For bodily discipline is only of little profit, but godliness is profitable for all things, since it holds promise for the present life and also for the life to come" (1 Tim. 4:8). "Your adornment must not be merely external—braiding the hair, and wearing gold jewelry, or putting on dresses; but let it be the hidden person of the heart, with the imperishable quality of a gentle and quiet spirit, which is precious in the sight of God" (1 Peter 3:3–4).

Please allow me to ask you some very penetrating, heart-searching questions at this point. Actually, all these questions relate to your own ultimate happiness.

- Do you really believe that money (or whatever else you love inordinately) can make you happier than these inner resources?[7]

7. If you coveted these treasures as much as you coveted money—if you spent half as much time, effort, and thought cultivating these inner resources as you spend cultivating material wealth—not only would you mortify your inordinate lust for money

- What is it that would make you happy?
- What are you waiting for to be happy (a spouse, power, friends, the approval of men, a different geographic location)?
- Would you really be happier if you had what you think would make you happier?
- If you think you would be happier, do you think the Lord is going to give you that desire *before* you learn to be content?

He has promised to provide not for all your wants but rather for your needs: "And my God will supply all your *needs* according to His riches in glory in Christ Jesus" (Phil. 4:19).

2. Contentment is realizing that true satisfaction can come only from building one's life around those things that cannot be taken away or destroyed.[8]

Jesus warned about the ephemeral nature of worldly possessions:

> Do not store up for yourselves treasures on earth, where moth and rust destroy, and where thieves break in and steal. But store up for yourselves treasures in heaven, where neither moth nor rust destroys, and where thieves do not break in or steal; for where your treasure is, there your heart will be also. (Matt. 6:19–21)

To put more stock in, to seek more pleasure in, to put more confidence in, or to place more value on temporal things than eternal ones is to set oneself up for tremendous dissatisfaction—if not utter devastation if those things are taken away (as by thieves)

and learn how to be content, but you would experience *far greater* happiness than all the money in the world could afford you.

8. The Institute in Basic Life Principles's definition for the character trait of *security* is "structuring my life around that which cannot be destroyed or taken away" (*Achieving True Success: How to Build Character as a Family* [Oklahoma City: International Association of Character Cities, 2006], 59).

or destroyed (as by rust). In fact, to love such temporal things inordinately (to covet them to the point of idolatry) is to invite discontentment and misery into your life.

On two different occasions in the New Testament, the apostle Paul linked covetousness to idolatry:

> For this you know with certainty, that no immoral or impure person or covetous man, who is an idolater, has an inheritance in the kingdom of Christ and God. (Eph. 5:5)

> Therefore consider the members of your earthly body as dead to immorality, impurity, passion, evil desire and greed, which amounts to idolatry. (Col. 3:5)

Much has been made lately about the addictive nature of people with various so-called psychological disorders. The truth is, we all have "addictive natures" in one way or another. This is so because we long for whatever brings us pleasure in ever-increasing measure. As Solomon put it:

> Sheol and Abaddon are never satisfied,
> > and never satisfied are the eyes of man. (Prov. 27:20 ESV)

> He who loves money will not be satisfied with money, nor he who loves abundance with its income. This too is vanity. (Eccl. 5:10)

When we go from longing for something to loving it, we are especially in danger of becoming in bondage ("addicted") to it. Now, temporal things (things that can be taken away or destroyed) are especially dangerous to become addicted to because if we love them (inordinately long for them), they will hurt us. The Bible speaks of those who love money, pleasure, preeminence, wine and oil, sleep, the world, and even their own lives (to name a few). But other things—eternal things—are fine to love because even if we are not satisfied with them and so long for more of them (even to the point of becoming addicted to them), we will suffer no harm. For example, the Bible encourages us to love Christ. Can too much love for him be a bad thing? Is he such a terrible thing to be addicted to? Can we love the Father too much?[9] The Bible also speaks of loving the written Word of God, of loving our neighbors, of loving wisdom, mercy, justice, and truth.[10]

3. Contentment is delighting in God more than in anything else.

The Protestant Reformer John Calvin referred to the human heart as a "perpetual factory of idols."[11] God has given us the ability to seek our happiness in anything we choose. We can delight in possessions, activities, ideas, money, pleasure, approval from others, our work, and even certain people. But Psalm 37:4 says, "Delight yourself [seek your happiness] in the LORD; and He will give you the desires of your heart." We may lawfully delight not only in the Lord but also in his Word, his will, his ways, and his wisdom (cf. 2 Chron. 17:6; Pss. 1:2; 40:8; Prov. 8:30). The problem comes when we either seek our happiness in those things God forbids or seek our happiness in lawful things (things that God allows) more than in him.

We know that it's wrong to seek our happiness in things that God expressly forbids—such as drunkenness, fornication, and marriage to an unbelieving spouse. But when we delight too much in those things that God allows (such as food, money, our jobs, leisure activities and avocations, or even the people we love), we can also be guilty of idolatry.

The question to ask yourself is: "In what do I delight?"

9. At this point, I am reminded of that old saying, "He is so heavenly minded that he is of no earthly good." The problem is that to be heavenly minded in the biblical sense is to be earthly good—to not be earthly good is to not be properly heavenly minded.

10. Many such good things are lawful for us to love because by virtue of their very "good" nature, they are self-limiting in preventing their own abuse.

11. John Calvin, *Institutes of the Christian Religion*, trans. Henry Beveridge (Edinburgh: The Edinburgh Printing Company, 1845), 1.11.8.

Personally, I delight in fishing, fly-fishing in particular. Is it a sin to seek a little bit of happiness in this way? Of course not! Everybody knows that fishing is the biblical sport. Some of the apostles were fishermen. (I even heard it said that John, the beloved apostle, was a fly-fisherman.) Fishing, then, is clearly *not* a sin. But what if, while fishing, I were to focus on the object of the delight and see God with only my peripheral vision, if at all? At that moment, my focus would be wrong, and I would be in danger of making my fishing an idol. If, on the other hand, I see the object of delight with my peripheral vision, all the while focusing on the gracious God who richly gives me all things to enjoy, and if I use the object as a means to praise my Creator, then I will be worshiping God in my heart rather than an idol.

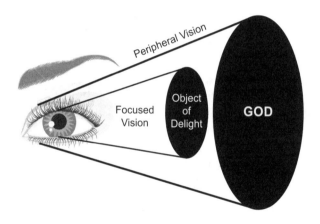

If, for example, while floating down the river, I am expressing my gratitude to God for his wonderful creation (the gorgeous countryside, the blue herons swooping across my path, the wood ducks flying overhead, and the beavers and squirrels scampering about), for the time off he has given me from work, for my unselfish wife, who does not complain about the time I spend recharging my emotional batteries by fishing, and for the fish he has allowed me to catch, then my fishing trip becomes a meaningful and genuine worship experience.

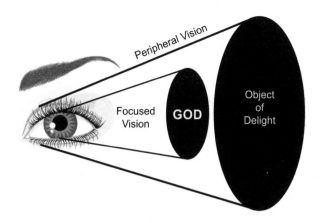

May I ask you another one of those probing questions? "What are you coveting to the point of idolatry?" If nothing comes to mind, I suggest that you run through the following checklist:

- ☐ Your money?
- ☐ Your pleasurable activities?
- ☐ Getting married?
- ☐ Your reputation?
- ☐ Control?
- ☐ Your space?
- ☐ Food?
- ☐ Having a boyfriend or girlfriend?
- ☐ Having a truly Christian marriage?
- ☐ Having a godly husband or wife?
- ☐ Your personal comfort?

"Perhaps I do have an idol or two. But how can I determine whether I've really made an idol out of one of these things you have suggested, or anything else, for that matter?"

The surest way I know to answer that question is with two other questions:

- Have you been willing to sin so that you can get what you want?

- Have you been willing to sin as a result of not being able to get what you want? (Do you become sinfully angry, hateful, vindictive, argumentative, impatient, unreasonable, irritable, critical, withdrawn, and so on when you are not able to have what you want?)

If the answer to either of these questions is "yes," then you wanted what you wanted *too much*. Perhaps you chose to do your own will rather than God's. Or maybe you used a privilege or pleasure that God gave you for his glory, and the benefit of others, exclusively for your own glory or benefit. If so, you are guilty of idolatry. The greater your frequency of sinning (either in an attempt to get what you want or as a result of not being able to get what you want), the greater your sin of idolatry.

If you answered "no" to the two previous questions (but are still uncertain about a possible idolatrous desire), here are a few more probing questions for you to consider. (Fill in as many blanks as you can; then prayerfully consider whether what you have identified is indeed an idol in your life.)

- What is it that I think I cannot be happy without?

_____

- What do I desire, long for, or crave?

_____

- What is it that I believe I must have?

_____

- What do I spend most of my spare thought time thinking about?

_____

- What do I worry most about losing?

_____

- In whom (or what) do I delight (seek my happiness) the most?

  _____

- What do I love more than I love God and my neighbor?

  _____

- What do I trust in more than God?

  _____

- What do I value the most?

  _____

- To whom do I pay the most honor and respect?

  _____

- To what (or whom) am I most devoted?

  _____

- On whom am I depending more than I depend on God?

  _____

- In what do I seek my refuge? (Where do I turn for relief?)

  _____

The next question you may want to consider is this: "What should I do if I have been guilty of idolatry?" or "How do I dethrone my idol?" The following outline may help you to formulate an initial answer. The last few pages of this booklet should provide you with additional weapons to supplement your arsenal for fighting against the sinful ruling motives of your heart.

(a) Ask the Lord to convict you of the sinfulness of your idolatrous desires.

   Search me, O God, and know my heart;
   Try me and know my anxious thoughts;

And see if there be any hurtful way in me,
And lead me in the everlasting way. (Ps. 139:23–24)

(b) Confess your culpability to God for breaking not only two of the Ten Commandments, but also Jesus' Great Commandment:

And God spoke all these words, saying:
"I am the LORD your God, who brought you out of the land of Egypt, out of the house of bondage.
"You shall have no other gods before Me.
"You shall not make for yourself any carved image, or any likeness of anything that is in heaven above, or that is in the earth beneath, or that is in the water under the earth; you shall not bow down to them nor serve them. For I, the LORD your God, am a jealous God, visiting the iniquity of the fathers on the children to the third and fourth generations of those who hate Me, but showing mercy to thousands, to those who love Me and keep My commandments." (Ex. 20:1–6 NKJV)

Then one of the scribes came, and having heard them reasoning together, perceiving that He had answered them well, asked Him, "Which is the first commandment of all?" Jesus answered him, "The first of all the commandments is: 'Hear, O Israel, the Lord our God, the Lord is one. And you shall love the Lord your God with all your heart, with all your soul, with all your mind, and with all your strength.' This is the first commandment." (Mark 12:28–30)

(c) Pray daily that God will help you to dethrone your idols and will give you a greater love for him than for anyone or anything else.

Who can discern his errors?
Declare me innocent from hidden faults.
Keep back your servant also from presumptuous sins;
let them not have dominion over me!

Then I shall be blameless,
>   and innocent of great transgression.

Let the words of my mouth and the meditation of my heart
>   be acceptable in your sight,
>   O LORD, my rock and my redeemer. (Ps. 19:12–14 ESV)

(d) Learn to view sinful anger, impatience, and anxiety as triggering a divinely installed smoke detector that lets you know when you are coveting something to the point of idolatry.

> What is the source of quarrels and conflicts among you? Is not the source your pleasures that wage war in your members? You lust and do not have; so you commit murder. You are envious and cannot obtain; so you fight and quarrel. You do not have because you do not ask. You ask and do not receive, because you ask with wrong motives, so that you may spend it on your pleasures. You adulteresses, do you not know that friendship with the world is hostility toward God? Therefore whoever wishes to be a friend of the world makes himself an enemy of God. (James 4:1–4)

(e) When your desires conflict with God's desires, choose to give God what he wants rather than giving yourself what you want.

> And He was saying, "Abba! Father! All things are possible for You; remove this cup from Me; yet not what I will, but what You will." (Mark 14:36)

4. Contentment is being able to adjust the level of one's desires to the condition and purpose chosen for him by God.

Paul learned an important element of contentment: the ability to regulate his level of desire to the circumstances into which God chose to place him from day to day:

I am not saying this because I am in need, for I have learned to be content whatever the circumstances. I know what it is to be in need, and I know what it is to have plenty. I have learned the secret of being content in any and every situation, whether well fed or hungry, whether living in plenty or in want. (Phil. 4:11–12 NIV)

One day, Paul might have been living in plenty; the next, he might have been living in want of something he had the day before. When it came to his temporal desires (wants, longings, and so forth), he was flexible.

Thomas Watson is again very helpful as he teaches us to regulate our fancy:

> It is the fancy which raises the price of things above their real worth. What is the reason one tulip is worth five pounds, another perhaps not worth one shilling? Fancy raises the price. The difference is rather imaginary than real. So, why should it be better to have thousands than hundreds? It is because men fancy it so. If we could fancy a lower condition better, as having less care in it, and less accountability, it would be far more desirable. The water that springs out of the rock drinks as sweet as if it came out of a golden chalice. Things are as we fancy them.
>
> Ever since the fall, the fancy is distempered. "God saw that the imagination of the thoughts of his heart were evil." Fancy looks through the wrong spectacles. Pray that God will sanctify your fancy. A lower condition would make us content if the mind and fancy were set correctly.[12]

What is the condition into which God has recently led you? What is God's purpose for your life right now? To what fancy are you having a difficult time adjusting?

Right now, in prayer, you can begin to adjust the level of your desires according to God's purpose for your life and the circum-

12. Thomas Watson, *The Art of Divine Contentment* (Morgan, PA: Soli Deo Gloria Publications, 2001), 126–27.

stances into which he has placed you. ("Lord, this is something that I want, but if it is not in accordance with your purposes for my life, please help me to be content without it. Teach me the right way to think about it.") Don't allow them to interfere with the divine program. Perhaps tomorrow your condition will be different. Perhaps tomorrow God will reveal other purposes for your life and ministry. Tomorrow he may give you the desires of your heart. But for today, work hard to turn down the thermostat on the temporal and turn up the register on the eternal.

We are indebted to Jeremiah Burroughs, the great Puritan author, who in his classic *The Rare Jewel of Christian Contentment* provides us with the next two definitions.

5. Contentment is willingly submitting to and delighting in God's wise and loving disposal in every condition of life.

> Then Job arose, tore his robe, and shaved his head; and he fell to the ground and worshiped. And he said:
>
> "Naked I came from my mother's womb,
> And naked shall I return there.
> The LORD gave, and the LORD has taken away;
> Blessed be the name of the LORD."
>
> In all this Job did not sin nor charge God with wrong.
> (Job 1:20–22 NKJV)

Job didn't blame his calamity on any of the immediate causes (the Sabeans, or the fire that fell from heaven, or the Chaldeans, or the great wind that came from across the wilderness, or the devil himself); rather, he saw God as the one who controlled all circumstances.

Burroughs develops this theme:

> The soul that has learned this lesson of contentment *looks up* to God in all things. He does not *look down* at the instruments and

means, so as to say that such a *man* did it, or that it was the unreasonableness of such and such *instruments*, or it was similar cruel treatment by so and so. But he *looks up* to God. A contented heart looks to God's disposal. That is, he sees the wisdom of God in everything. In his submission to God, he sees His sovereignty, but what enables him to take pleasure [in the trial] is God's wisdom. The Lord knows how to order things better than I. The Lord sees further ahead than I do. I see only the present but the Lord sees a great while from now. And how do I know but that had it not been for this affliction, I should have been undone. I know that the love of God may as well stand with an afflicted condition as with a prosperous condition. There are reasonings of this kind in a contented spirit, submitting to the disposal of God.[13]

Your current circumstances didn't take God by surprise. In fact, God, in his infinite wisdom and love, is providentially at work in them. The sooner you submit to his sovereign will[14] in this matter, the sooner you will be able to overcome discontentment and much of the misery associated with it.

Here is the bottom line (in terms of how we should think about our desires): "When I have employed and exhausted all biblical means to obtain what I want, I must assume that it is not God's will for me to have it right now.[15] And I will be thankful for and contented with his present purposes for my life rather than murmur and complain about them."

6. Contentment is knowing how to use the things of the world without being engrossed in them.

The apostle Paul exhorted the saints at Corinth,

13. Jeremiah Burroughs, *The Rare Jewel of Christian Contentment* (Mulberry, IN: Sovereign Grace Publishers, 2001), 10 (paraphrased).

14. I make a distinction between God's revealed will, which is found in Scripture, and his decreed will, which sometimes includes giving others the freedom to sin against him. Christ's redemptive work on the cross, which God ordained in eternity past, involved certain individuals' committing murder: "Him, being delivered by the determined purpose and foreknowledge of God, you have taken by lawless hands, have crucified, and put to death" (Acts 2:23 NKJV).

15. (If at all!)

But this I say, brethren, the time is short, so that from now on even those who have wives should be as though they had none, those who weep as though they did not weep, those who rejoice as though they did not rejoice, those who buy as though they did not possess, and those who use this world as not misusing it. For the form of this world is passing away. (1 Cor. 7:29–31 NKJV)

Paul is addressing some questions the Corinthians had about marriage. In light of the "present distress" (which some believe is the coming[16] persecution of the church by the Emperor Nero), he urges unmarried individuals to remain single if at all possible. Part of his argument has to do with not getting too attached to the comforts of this world. Once again, Jeremiah Burroughs hits the bull's-eye:

Do not be inordinately taken up with the comforts of this world when you have them. When you have them, do not take too much satisfaction in them. There is a certain principle: However inordinate any man or woman is in sorrow when a comfort has been taken from them, so were they inordinate in their rejoicing in the comfort when they had it. For instance, God takes away a child and you are inordinately sorrowful, beyond what God allows in a natural or Christian way. Now although I never knew before how your heart was towards the child, yet when I see this, though you are a stranger to me, I may without breach of charity conclude that your heart was immoderately set upon your child or husband, or upon any other comfort that I see you grieving [inordinately] for when God has taken it away. If you hear bad news about your estates, and your hearts are dejected immoderately, and you have a discontented mood because of such and such a trial, certainly your hearts were immoderately set upon the world. So, likewise, for your reputation, if you hear others report this or that evil about you, and your hearts are dejected because you think you suffer in your name, your

16. Paul may have been speaking as a prophet, warning of the terrible persecution that Nero was about to inflict on Christians. At the time he was writing, the persecution was in its inception.

hearts were inordinately set upon your name and reputation. Now therefore, the way for you to not be immoderate in your sorrow when afflictions come is to not be immoderate in your love and delights when you have prosperity.[17]

Have you allowed yourself to be preoccupied with the comforts of this life? Do you view the things God has given you to enjoy as a means to an end (to glorify God) or as an end in and of themselves (your personal pleasure)? What has the Lord given you to use?

Put a check next to the things below with which you are most tempted to become engrossed:

☐ Your wealth   ☐ Your time   ☐ Your talents and
☐ Your good looks ☐ Your reputation   abilities
☐ Your spiritual   ☐ Your hobbies   ☐ Your home
  gifts   ☐ Your spouse   ☐ Your children
☐ Your clothing   ☐ Your authority

Why do you suppose the Lord has given you these things to enjoy? Richard Baxter has some insight into the answer to this vital question:

> Remember to what ends all worldly things were made and given you. . . . They are the provender of our bodies; our traveling furniture and helps; our inns, and solacing company in the way; they are some of God's love-tokens, some of the lesser pieces of his coin, and bear his image and superscription. They are drops from the rivers of the eternal pleasures; to tell the mind by the way of the senses how good the Donor is, and how amiable; and what higher delights there are for souls; and to point us to the better things which these foretell. They are messengers from heaven, to testify our Father's care and love, and to bespeak our thankfulness,

17. Burroughs, *The Rare Jewel of Christian Contentment*, 226 (paraphrased).

love, and duty; and to bear witness against sin, and bind us faster to obedience. . . . They are the tools by which we must do much of our Master's work. They are means by which we may refresh our brethren, and express our love to one another, and our love to our Lord and Master in his servants. They are our Master's stock, which we must trade with. . . . These are the uses to which God gives us outward mercies. Love them thus, and delight in them, and use them thus, and spare not; yea, seek them thus, and be thankful for them. But when the creatures are given for so excellent a use, will you debase them all by making them only the fuel of your lusts, and the provisions for your flesh? And will you love them, and dote upon them in these base respects; while you utterly neglect their noblest use?[18]

7. Contentment is thanking God even in circumstances in which one used to murmur and complain.

Here is the *short* test for discontentment: How often do you murmur or complain? We are commanded to "do all things without grumbling or disputing" (Phil. 2:14). We could even say that murmuring and complaining is another "biblical opposite" for contentment (see Ex. 16:1–4; Num. 11:4–6).

We are also commanded to give thanks in every circumstance. "In everything give thanks; for this is God's will for you in Christ Jesus" (1 Thess. 5:18). So thankfulness is a powerful antidote for discontentment (and for murmuring and complaining).

Putting this characterization of contentment into practice will require you to *learn* how to interpret providence (especially smaller, more mundane providences) in the light of God's sovereignty and goodness (in other words, to learn to *see* providence; see Rom. 8:28). Paul used the word *learned* twice in reference to contentment:

18. Richard Baxter, "A Christian Directory," *The Practical Works of Richard Baxter*, vol. 1 (London: George Virtue, 1838), 220.

Not that I speak from want, for *I have learned* to be content in whatever circumstances I am. I know how to get along with humble means, and I also know how to live in prosperity; in any and every circumstance *I have learned* the secret of being filled and going hungry, both of having abundance and suffering need. (Phil. 4:11–12)

Someone has noted that contentment is contrary to human nature and must be learned:

We long for a better environment in which to live, assuming that with it we will achieve contentment. Yet Adam and Eve had the perfect environment . . . perfect health, a perfect marriage, a perfect garden, and daily fellowship with God Himself, yet they soon believed the lie that God had not provided everything they needed for their present and future happiness.

If Adam and Eve were not content in the Garden of Eden, what hope is there for the rest of us, apart from the spiritual insight that comes from God?[19]

A good example of someone who had to learn this lesson is the patriarch Joseph. We sometimes think that when he was sold into slavery by his brothers, he had the same confident attitude that he had years later when he said to them, "You meant evil against me, but God meant it for good" (Gen. 50:20). The truth is, however, that he had more to learn about the perfections of God and was not quite so cool, calm, and collected as we might have thought: "Then they said to one another, 'Truly we are guilty concerning our brother, because we saw the distress of his soul when he pleaded with us, yet we would not listen; therefore this distress has come upon us'" (Gen. 42:21).

19. Character Council of Indiana, Inc., March 2003 Biblical Character Study, available at http://www.charactercouncil.org/resources/biblicalstudies/Contentment%20 Bulletin.PDF.

Suggestions for Developing Contentment

Here are a few practical things you might find helpful as, by God's grace, you seek to replace covetousness with contentment:

1. Be sure you truly understand the nature and scope of your own covetousness.

Ask the Lord to convict you of the sinfulness of your idolatrous desires.

> Search me, O God, and know my heart;
> Try me and know my anxious thoughts;
> And see if there be any hurtful way in me,
> And lead me in the everlasting way. (Ps. 139:23–24)

If you haven't yet done so, take the Biblical Contentment Inventory beginning on page 7 of this booklet. Memorize and meditate on each of the aforementioned definitions of *contentment* (and the associated Scripture passages) that most directly relate to your style of coveting.

2. Pray daily that God would help you dethrone your idolatrous desires and give you a greater love for him than for anyone or anything else.

> The law of the LORD is perfect,
>   reviving the soul;
> the testimony of the LORD is sure,
>   making wise the simple;
> the precepts of the LORD are right,
>   rejoicing the heart;
> the commandment of the LORD is pure,
>   enlightening the eyes;
> the fear of the LORD is clean,
>   enduring forever;
> the rules of the LORD are true,
>   and righteous altogether.

More to be desired are they than gold,
  even much fine gold;
sweeter also than honey
  and drippings of the honeycomb.
Moreover, by them is your servant warned;
  in keeping them there is great reward. (Ps. 19:7–11 ESV)

3. Train yourself to thank and praise the Lord when first tempted to murmur and complain.

The example is Job, who, after losing so much, immediately went into worship mode. Jeremiah Burroughs makes a great point about worship and contentment:

> You worship God more by contentment than when you come to hear a sermon, or spend a half an hour, or an hour in prayer, or when you come to receive a sacrament. These are acts of God's worship, but they are only external acts of worship—to hear and pray and receive sacraments. But [contentment] is the soul's worship—to subject itself in this way to God. . . . In active obedience we worship God by doing what pleases God, but in passive obedience we also worship God by being pleased with what He does.[20]

You may find it helpful to develop a portable "thankfulness list" that you can take out and review when you first realize that you have slipped back into discontented thinking. The back of this booklet contains a few worksheets that you can use to begin formulating your own list of things for which you may be thankful.

4. Remember that your greatest needs cannot be met by temporal pleasures.

We are indebted to Richard Baxter for this nugget:

20. Burroughs, *The Rare Jewel of Christian Contentment*, 120 (paraphrased).

Strive to comprehend your greatest needs, which worldly wealth will not supply. You have sinned against God and money will not buy your pardon. You have incurred His displeasure, and money will not reconcile Him to you. You are condemned to everlasting misery by the law, and money will not pay the ransom. You are dead in sin, and polluted, and captivated by the flesh, and money will sooner increase your bondage than it will deliver you. Your conscience is ready to tear your heart for your willful folly and contempt of grace, and money will not bribe it to be quiet. Judas brought back his money, and hanged himself, once his conscience was awakened. Money will not enlighten a blinded man, nor soften a hard heart, nor humble a proud heart, nor justify a guilty soul. It will not keep away a fever or tuberculosis, nor ease the gout, or kidney stone or toothache. It will not keep off ghastly death—but die you must, even if you have all the world. Look up to God, and remember that you are entirely in His hands; and consider whether He will love or favor you for your wealth. Look to the Day of Judgment and consider whether there money will help you out, or the rich will do better than the poor.[21]

5. Make good interpretations of God's dealings with you.

In 1 Corinthians 13:7, we read that love "believes all things." That means that we are to believe the best about others. In other words, if there are ten possible interpretations or explanations as to why someone took a particular course of action, nine of them being evil and only one of them being good, the loving person will, in the absence of real evidence to the contrary, choose to reject the bad and believe the good. Now, if we are commanded to view other sinners with this kind of optimism, how much more should we put the best possible interpretation on *God's* dealings with us? How much more should we forsake the bad interpretations of his providence in our lives and accept the good ones?

21. Richard Baxter, *Christian Directory*, 218 (paraphrased).

He who comes to God must believe not only that he exists, but also that "He is a rewarder of those who seek Him" (Heb. 11:6). Jeremiah Burroughs developed this theme:

Make a good interpretation of God's ways toward you. If any good interpretation can be made of God's ways toward you, *make it!* You would think it to be a big deal (you would take it rather badly), if you had a friend who always made bad interpretations of your ways toward him. If you should attempt to converse with people who didn't speak your language, but who interpreted your attempts to do so in the worst possible light, you would think their company to be very tedious. It is very tedious to the spirit of God when we make such bad interpretations of His ways towards us.

When God deals with us differently than we would like, we will see it in the worst light rather than best. So, when some affliction comes to you, many good senses may be made of God's dealings with you. You should think, "It may be that the Lord intends only to test me through this. Or, perhaps He saw that my heart was too preoccupied with something that He provided for me, so he intends to show me the sinfulness of my heart. Perhaps, God saw that if my wealth continued, I would fall into sin, or that the better my position were to be, the worse my soul would be. Or better yet, it may be that God intends to use this affliction to somehow bless me— perhaps even to prepare me for some wonderful ministry (or achievement) which He has ordained for me." This is how you should reason.

But we, on the other hand, make bad interpretations of such providences and say, "God doesn't intend good to come of this—surely He intends to manifest His wrath and displeasure towards me. This is just another in a long line of difficulties He is going to fling on me." Just as they did in the wilderness you say to yourselves, "God has brought us here to slay us." This is the worst interpretation you could possibly make of God's ways. Why would you make these "worst case" interpretations when there are better ones that could be made?

In 1 Corinthians 13, when the Scripture speaks of love, it says, "Love doesn't think evil."[22] Love is of that nature that if ten interpretations of a matter may be made—nine of them bad and one of them good—love will take (believe) the one that is good and leave (disbelieve) the nine. So, if ten interpretations about God's ways toward you may be presented to you, and if only one of them is good, and the other nine are bad, you should accept the one that is good, and reject the other nine.

I implore you to consider that God doesn't deal with you the way that you deal with Him. Should He make the worst interpretation of all of your dealings with Him the way that you do of His toward you, it would be very unpleasant for you.[23]

6. Consider food, clothing, and shelter your only temporal necessities.

As Christians, we should be thankful for these necessities. Any temporal gifts above and beyond these are a bonus for which we should be especially grateful. If we were truly grateful for all the "bonuses" that we have all been given, we would not struggle with being discontent. You may find a couple of passages especially helpful as you consider this point:

> But godliness actually is a means of great gain when accompanied by contentment. For we have brought nothing into the world, so we cannot take anything out of it either. If we have food and covering, with these we shall be content. (1 Tim. 6:6–8)

> Look at the birds of the air, that they do not sow, nor reap nor gather into barns, and yet your heavenly Father feeds them. Are you not worth much more than they? And who of

---

22. The same portion also says that love "believes all things" (that is, it believes the best about another).

23. Burroughs, *The Rare Jewel of Christian Contentment*, 223–24 (modernized).

you by being worried can add a single hour to his life? And why are you worried about clothing? Observe how the lilies of the field grow; they do not toil nor do they spin, yet I say to you that not even Solomon in all his glory clothed himself like one of these. But if God so clothes the grass of the field, which is alive today and tomorrow is thrown into the furnace, will He not much more clothe you? You of little faith! Do not worry then, saying, "What will we eat?" or "What will we drink?" or "What will we wear for clothing?" For the Gentiles eagerly seek all these things; for your heavenly Father knows that you need all these things. But seek first His kingdom and His righteousness, and all these things will be added to you. (Matt. 6:26–33)

Notice the connection Jesus makes between those who serve money and those who are overly concerned (worried) about *food* and *clothing*:

No man can serve two masters: for either he will hate the one, and love the other; or else he will hold to the one, and despise the other. *Ye cannot serve God and mammon.* Therefore I say unto you, Take no thought for your life, what ye shall eat, or what ye shall drink; nor yet for your body, what ye shall put on. Is not the life more than meat, and the body than raiment? (Matt. 6:24–25 KJV)

If you are *discontent* with *having only* food and clothing, you will soon begin to worry about *having enough* food and clothing.

Try to look at it this way: There are at least two antithetical concepts to the love of money in the Bible. One is *discontentment*; the other is *worry* (see Matt. 6:19–24). To the extent that discontentment and worry are both dissimilar to the love of money, they are both also similar to each other. They are both sinful attitudes. Discontentment is *not being satisfied* with the food and clothing that God has provided. (Specifically, being *sinfully* dissatisfied. There is a difference between desiring to improve one's own estate by pursuing a better job or education, and being so dissatisfied that one will pursue these things at the expense of God's glory—will pursue them, in other words, by sinning.) Worry is *not being confident* that God is going to provide food and clothing.

Remember also that God has promised to provide for your needs and that if you walk uprightly, you will not lack any good thing:

> And my God will supply all your needs according to His riches in glory in Christ Jesus. (Phil. 4:19)

> For the Lord God is a sun and shield;
> The Lord gives grace and glory;
> No good thing does He withhold from those who walk uprightly.
> (Ps. 84:11)

7. Develop the mind-set of a soldier.

Paul admonished Timothy with these words:

> Suffer hardship with me, as a good soldier of Christ Jesus. No soldier in active service entangles himself in the affairs of everyday life, so that he may please the one who enlisted him as a soldier. (2 Tim. 2:3–4)

Thomas Watson reminded his readers:

> We are in a military condition—we are soldiers—and a soldier is content with anything. So what if he doesn't have his stately house, his rich furniture, and his soft bed—he can lie on straw as well as on down. He doesn't think about his lodging. Rather his thoughts run to dividing the spoil, and the garland of honor that shall be placed upon his head. And in light of this hope, he is content to face any danger, and endure any hardship. A Christian is a military person. He fights the Lord's battles.

He is Christ's sign bearer. So what if he endures hard times and the bullets fly about? He fights for a crown and therefore must be content.[24]

8. Do not set your heart on the temporal comforts and pleasures that God allows you to enjoy.

In the Psalms we are warned, "If riches increase, do not set your heart upon them" (Ps. 62:10). Those of us who "have been raised up with Christ" are rather to "keep seeking the things above, where Christ is, seated at the right hand of God. *Set your mind* on the things above, not on the things that are on earth" (Col. 3:1–2). What does it mean to set one's heart or mind on something? It means to seek, to direct one's mind toward, or even to keep thinking about that object. The idea is to focus our minds on Christ and his eternal heavenly kingdom (rather than on our own temporal earthly one).

9. Remember that the more you have, the greater will be your degree of accountability.

So much can be gained in our battles against discontentment (and covetousness) by thinking about heaven. This subject deserves an entire booklet all its own, but for now, consider the words of Jesus: "From everyone who has been given much, much will be required; and to whom they entrusted much, of him they will ask all the more" (Luke 12:48). Here is an exercise you might want to try. Make a list of your top three temporal pleasures. Then write out a paragraph for each one (as a sort of trial run) as to what you might say to the Lord when asked by him to give an account for them. And, if you are prone to spend too much time thinking about ("obsessing" over) one particular temporal delight, why not spend a day investing as much time (minute for minute) thinking

24. Watson, *The Art of Divine Contentment*, 99 (paraphrased).

about how you will give account for that delight as you invest in taking pleasure in it?

Learning to be content isn't easy. But it can be done. And in the final analysis, it is *easier* than being discontent. May God give you the eyes to see that he has already provided everything you need to glorify him and enjoy him forever.

> "Instead of complaining at his lot, a contented man is thankful that his condition and circumstances are no worse than they are. Instead of greedily desiring something more than the supply of his present need, he rejoices that God still cares for him. Such an one is 'content' with such as he has."
>
> —Arthur W. Pink[25]

25. *Comfort for Christians* (Mulberry, IN: Sovereign Grace Publishers, 2007), 74.

Thankfulness List

With what am I currently discontent?

_____

_____

For what may I offer up thanksgiving to God?

_____

_____

_____

_____

_____

_____

_____

_____

_____

_____

_____

_____

_____

_____

_____

Thankfulness List

With what am I currently discontent?

_____

_____

For what may I offer up thanksgiving to God?

_____

_____

_____

_____

_____

_____

_____

_____

_____

_____

_____

_____

_____

_____

_____

_____

_____

Thankfulness List

With what am I currently discontent?

_____

_____

For what may I offer up thanksgiving to God?

_____

_____

_____

_____

_____

_____

_____

_____

_____

_____

_____

_____

_____

_____

_____

_____